Connemara Pony Handbook

Niamh O'Dochartaigh

Published by Árdcrú Books

Connemara Pony Handbook

by

Niamh O'Dochartaigh

Cover and text illustrations by Eavan O'Dochartaigh

Layout and Design by Lisa Rodgers

PUBLISHED BY ÁRDCRÚ BOOKS

Printed by Clodóirí Lurgan Teo, Galway

ISBN no. 978-0-9555100-0-7

Acknowledgements

I wish to thank sincerely all of the following people who helped to make the book possible. They supplied photos, information and valuable advice and encouragement and to them I am deeply indebted: They are

The Connemara Pony Breeders Society, Carol Bradbury, Bobby and Kevin Bolger, Stephanie Brooks and Pony Club Instructors at Errislannon Riding Centre, Anne Brennan, Bernie Brennan, Ciaran Briscoe, Joe Burke, Jimmy Canavan, Judy Cazabon and Siobhan Sullivan at Cleggan Bay Riding Centre, Josie Conroy, James de Courcey, Ciaran Curran, Willie Diamond, Marynell Eyles, Robbie and Barbara Fallon, Deirdre Feeley, Bernard Finneran, Paddy Geoghegan and Joan Geoghegan, Joe, John and Malachy Gorham, Eamon Hannan, Joan Hawkins, Padraig and Nicola Heanue, Lady Anne Hemphill, Padraig Hynes, Bridie Lally, Patricia Lalor, Lady Maria Levinge, Angela Lupton, Pat Lyne, Mary McCann, Kirstin McDonagh, Tomás MacLochlainn, John McLoughlin, Veterinary Surgeon Philip McManus and son John, Eddie Madden, Mary Mitchell, John Noel Mullen, Michael Mulligan, Ann and Eavan Murphy, Gabriel Murphy, Nicola Musgrave, Martin Naughton, Val Noone, Dan O'Brien, Ursula O'Brolcháin Ellis, Eithne O'Connell, Sandra O'Donnell at Moycullen Riding Centre, Frank O'Malley, Henry O'Toole, Elizabeth Petch, Juliet Perrin, Ruth Rogers, Carmel Santry, Carole Seigne, Sean Stagg, John Varley

My husband Eoin and my family gave me every support and help along the way and to them and especially to my daughter Eavan, who did the illustrations, and to Aideen who advised on content and to Niall and Conor who provided moral support, many, many thanks.

EAVAN '06

Contents

Foreword

I am delighted to welcome Niamh Ó Dochartaigh's third book, Connemara Pony Handbook. At a time when many Connemara ponies are being used in the performance arena it is opportune that we would have a book like this.

The book is aimed at the first-time buyer and there has never been as many of these as in recent years. It begins with a concise history of the pony, tracing its development from the beginning some centuries ago to the foundation of the Connemara Pony Breeders Society in 1923 and through the twentieth century to the present day.

The main section deals with the nuts and bolts of owning and performing with a Connemara pony. It is full of interesting and wise nuggets of information and advice which will be invaluable to young and old alike. It deals with every aspect from finding the right pony, buying tack, taking lessons and going to shows.

People will love the picture gallery at the end. There are shots of ponies and characters, many of which appear in print for the first time which will delight and fascinate the reader.

A very beautiful feature of the book are the pen and ink watercolours by Eavan Ó Dochartaigh

Tréaslaím le Niamh Ó Dochartaigh as ucht an obair chruinn thuiscineach atá déanta anseo aice. Léiríonn sí a saineolas féin agus roineann sí é le glún nua a bhainfidh taitneamh agus tairbhe as.

'Sé seo an chéad leabhar faoin gcapaillín a phléann cúrsaí marcaíochta agus atá dírithe ar an aos óg.

Fáiltím roimhe agus molaim go hard é.

Tomás MacLochlainn
President Connemara Pony Breeders Society

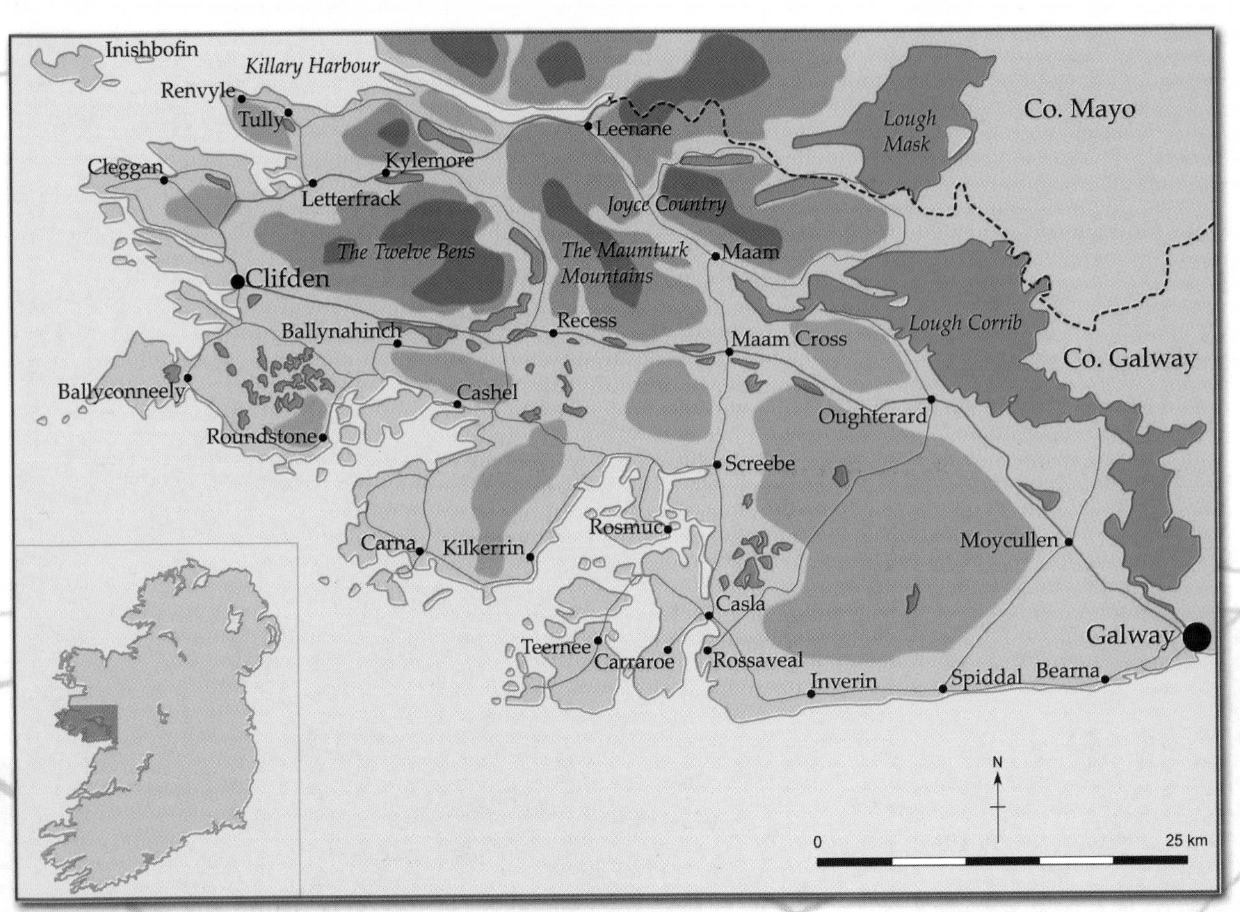

Connemara Location Map

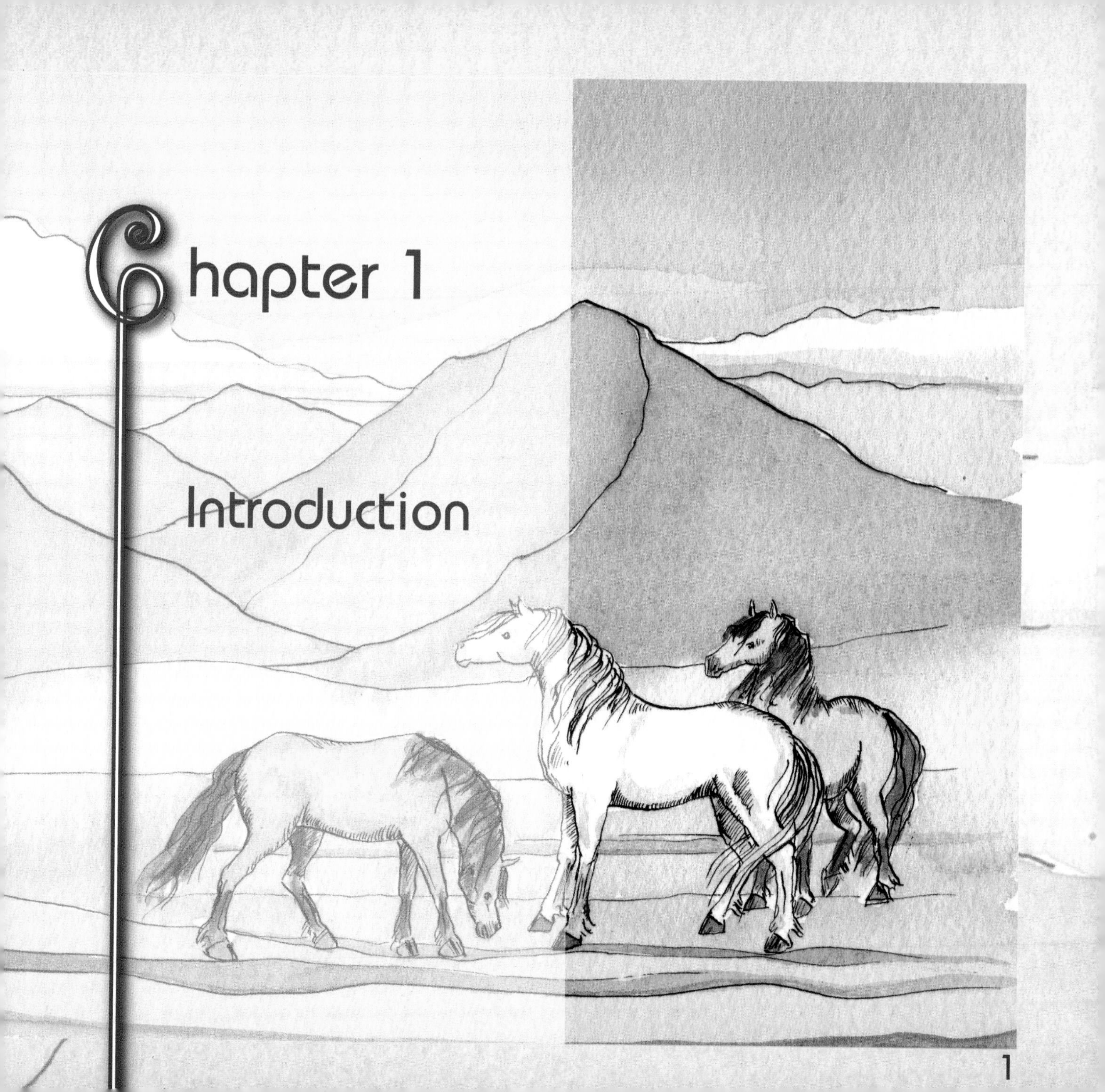

Chapter 1

Introduction

Chapter 1

The annual Connemara Pony Show in Clifden is the largest gathering anywhere in the world of Ireland's distinctive native pony.

Every year on the 3rd Thursday in August you will see these ponies; mares with their foals, yearlings, two year old fillies and colts, mature mares, geldings and splendid stallions as well as ridden Connemaras, gathered together in their native territory.

This spectacular homeland, a wilderness of mountains, lakes, bogs, rocky moorland and pounding Atlantic waves, lies in the most westerly part of Ireland. The Connemara Pony lovers who flock to Clifden from all corners of the globe in Show Week, add to the unique atmosphere for which this Show is renowned.

Origins

The Connemara Pony of today has come a long way from its mysterious and uncharted beginnings when wild herds roamed the sparsely inhabited landscape, long before tracks or roads made access to its interior a possibility. This magnificent but harshly unforgiving terrain, swept by gales and rain, made for the evolution of a tough, hardy, sure-footed animal with the resilience to survive and move with speed and agility, whether in boggy soil or on rough stony ground. The environment also produced a pony which had to be a good forager, finding food and shelter on barren mountainside and sandy seashore.

Main Ring Clifden, four and five year old mares

Three year old fillies line-up at Clifden

Show jumping for Ireland in Verona, Italy, *Sillogue Darkie* by *Ard Talisman-Coillchrú Esmerelda*, rider David Blake, owner Ciaran Briscoe

Herd of ponies in a mountain valley

From small Celtic horses to tall elegant Arabs imported in Spanish galleons over the seas, to the later Welsh, Thoroughbred and Draught blood introduced by landowners and breeders, the pony over time became a fusion of some of the best and the worst of imported blood.

The Connemara Breeders Society was formed in 1923 and proceeded to breed in a more orderly way from the best of the native stallions and mares. Their aim was to salvage the remnants of the good native type of pony, one renowned as a strong, hardy animal with both endurance and quality in its conformation and temperament.

Today the Connemara pony has successfully adapted to a transformed lifestyle. Breeders Societies exist in over15 countries and the pony is shown, ridden and much valued as a leisure and competition pony in many parts of the world. From its humble beginnings, this pony is now bringing enjoyment and pleasure to countless owners and riders worldwide

Its modern lifestyle is a far cry from the simpler yet far harsher lifestyle of the pre-historic ancestors and is also very different from the life of the working pony of the nineteenth and early twentieth centuries.

Let us take a brief look back at what life might have been like for both owners and ponies in previous ages.

Chapter 2

Water Horses, myth and legend

Chapter 2

The sea is a constant presence in many parts of Connemara. It winds its way far inland in many bays, ragged inlets and gulfs, and the hinterland valleys and blanket bogs are dotted with lakes and fast flowing rivers. Water is such an enduring presence here that it is not surprising to find that many fanciful tales, embellished no doubt by successive storytellers, survive from Celtic mythology and folklore.

In Celtic pagan Ireland there was no clear dividing line between the natural and the supernatural, between the actual world and the Otherworld, often seen as the land of happiness, over the water to the west of Ireland. Horses enjoyed an exalted position in old Irish society and in a pre-Christian land where water was believed to be the gateway to the Otherworld, an oral tradition existed throughout Ireland connecting the horse to this Otherworld. Fables tell of horses which emerge mysteriously from sea, lakes and rivers, spend some time in human ownership and eventually vanish into the misty depths once more..

The master of all sea creatures, Manannán Mac Lir, was believed to travel the waves mounted on a powerful grey horse that was a symbol of the magical powers of both horse and rider. Manannán, also a sun god, was sometimes seen as having the form of a horse.

There are tales of Oisín, a warrior of the Fianna, who is invited to Tir na nÓg, the land of eternal youth, by Niamh Chinn Óir (Niamh of the golden hair) and travels with her on her white steed across the western waves. Three hundred years later, he arrives back in Ireland and falls to earth from his magic spirit-horse, who gallops away through the surf. His vital link with the Otherworld gone, Oisin is immediately transformed into an old man, and

Sea God Mannanán Mac Lir

Connemara landscape

Niamh Cinn Óir and Oisín

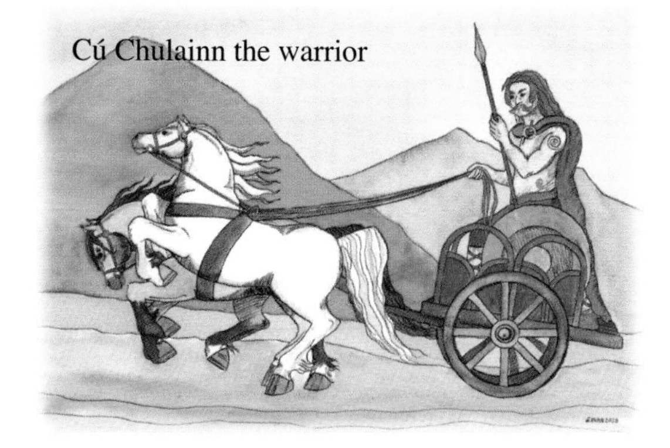
Cú Chulainn the warrior

Quartzite stone overlooking Ballinakill Bay

Tulira Mairtín by *Tooreen Ross-Glen Nelly,* breeder/owner Lord Hemphill

finds himself frail, friendless and unknown in a much changed land.

Another fable tells of the twin horses of the Red Branch Knights' hero Cú Chulainn. Born on the same day as the young warrior, these small horses pull his war-chariot and are invincible on the field of battle, but they too return to water and the Otherworld after the death of their young master.

These fairy animals were said to leave the human world either on the death of their owner or if treated harshly in this world. A story illustrating this belief comes from Moyard in north Connemara and tells of a white horse which once emerged from the mists of Garranbaun Lake. A local man manages to catch, halter and saddle him, jumps on his back and rides him furiously over the surrounding hills, before dismounting and hanging the saddle on a white standing stone that is still visible on top of one of these hills. The horse gallops back to the lake and is submerged in its depths, never to be seen again, having obviously had enough of its harsh rider, and making the choice to return to its former existence.

In more recent folklore the handsome under-water resident stallion, known as the 'each uisce' or water horse, was said to emerge from a lake on nights of a full moon to graze on the lakeshore, and on occasion to cover local mares and produce high-quality foals for the lucky small-farming owners.

Nowadays, the mystical aura which surrounded the horse has faded but that same value, esteem, and affection which our ancestors felt for their small native ponies is still present today in the hearts of many who love the animal for its beauty, its strength and above all its brave spirit.

Chapter 3

The Celtic horse and Arab blood

There is archaeological evidence to show that horses existed in Ireland in prehistoric times, as the bones of small horses and the remains of chariots dated from before 2000 BC have been found at sites such as Newgrange and Loughrea in County Galway. The Celtic people brought the Gaelic language and also their small dun ponies and chariots with them as they fled from the Roman takeover in England and Wales in the 3rd century B.C. Over time the Celtic horses bred and blended with the original native breed.

12th century stone carved horseman from Teaglach Éinne,Aran

Dept of the Environment, Heritage and Local Government

Spanish influence

The romantic tale is still told of Andalusian stallions that swam ashore and ran with the native herds, swimming from ships of the ill-fated Spanish Armada, wrecked off the treacherous rocks of the Galway coast in 1588. This story harks back to the mythical Otherworld water-horse fables of an earlier age but in actual fact many Spanish and Arab horses had arrived on Irish soil before the Armada disaster. In the early Middle Ages small horses from Asturia in north-west Spain were known to have been imported to Ireland.

Irish chieftain in full dress with horse-boy and servant. Image of Irelande, John Derricke 1581

National Library of Ireland

Wealthy Galway merchants in the 16th century liked to import Arab horses

Many Connemara ponies have an Arab look *Village Belle*

It is recorded that ships trading between the port of Galway and Spain between the 13th and the 16th centuries often carried Arab and Barb horses which had come from North Africa. It appears that these fine animals had become popular with wealthy Galway merchants.

The Viking and Norman invasions seemed not to have affected the type of Irish hobbie (as they were called) which remained popular as a means of transport throughout the west of Ireland in particular, although gradually larger types of horses became commonly used in other parts of Ireland.

By the early 19th Century, the building of roads in Connemara had encouraged some landlords to settle in the area and Arab colts were imported by the Martins of Ballinahinch, and the Blakes at Renvyle among others and these were mated with local mares.

It is no surprise to see that many Connemara ponies of today still carry the head of their Arab forebears.

Orphans in Famine years.
National Library of Ireland

Chapter 4

Famine and Poverty

Chapter 4

Carrying out the dead

The extreme hardship and misery of Famine times in mid-nineteenth century Connemara caused people to abandon their poor smallholdings, either to emigrate to a better life in America, or as so often happened, to die in conditions of appalling poverty at home.

Poverty and desperation gripped the land. Smallholders and their families could no longer afford to keep their animals, and the ponies were probably the first of the stock to be sold off. The importing of Arab stallions came to an end as big landowners also went bankrupt.

The breeding of the Connemara pony was certainly not a priority and it is likely that a number of ponies reverted to their wild state and the resulting indiscriminate breeding weakened the breed. Donkeys took their place as the small farmer's beast of burden during and after the hungry years.

Congested Districts Board members visit Connemara circa 1900

The Connemara Pony in decline

In the late nineteenth century, the Government of the day took steps to help the people of Connemara to recover from the famine years and to enable them to gain a livelihood. The Congested Districts Board was set up and proceeded to build roads, bridges and harbours as well as giving aid to fishing, agriculture and cottage industries. One of their aims was the improvement of all breeds of all livestock, including the weakened native breed of pony.

Various types of stallions were introduced to the area; Thoroughbred, Hackney, Welsh Cob, and Arab stallions were among the more usual types to be sent to various outposts to service the local mares. Not all of these had a good effect on the development of the native pony;

The stylish hackney of the late C19

Michael O'Malley from Rosmuc

'*The Irish Dragoon*' one of two Connemara ponies that represented the breed at the Olympia Rare Breeds Parade of 1912

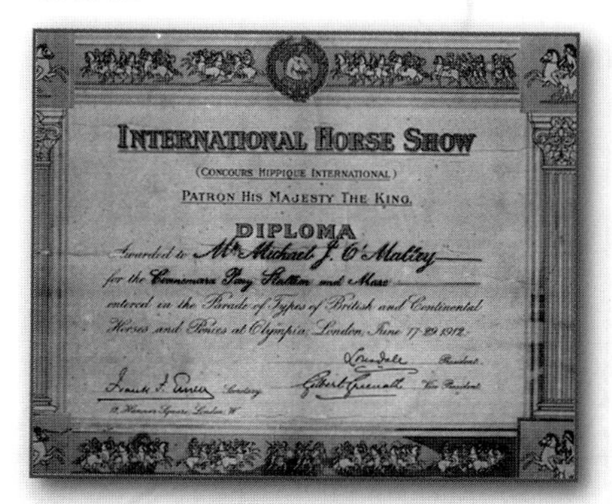

INTERNATIONAL HORSE SHOW

(CONCOURS HIPPIQUE INTERNATIONAL)

PATRON HIS MAJESTY THE KING.

DIPLOMA

Awarded to Mr Michael J. O'Malley

for the Connemara Pony Stallion and Mare

entered in the Parade of Types of British and Continental Horses and Ponies at Olympia, London, June 17-29 1912.

President.

Secretary. Vice President.

The Olympia Diploma received by Michael O'Malley

in particular the hackney's high trotting movement was particularly unsuited to the rocky and wet bog terrain of Connemara. However, despite the efforts of the Board, and indeed partly due to their efforts, by the early twentieth Century the traditional Connemara Pony breed was threatened with extinction.

Revival

A new era commenced when a public debate concerning the pony was sparked by a breeder from Ros Muc in South Connemara. Michael O'Malley kept work-ponies and like everyone else in those days, he rode them as a means of transport wherever his business took him. All journeys were made on horseback or in traps and sidecars.

He felt so strongly about the need to preserve the traditional pony type that he accepted an invitation--secured for him by a London physician and horseman, who became friendly with Michael on fishing trips to Screeb –to show the ponies at the Rare Breeds Parade at the Olympia Horse Show of 1912.

Michael then undertook a most daunting journey with two of his ponies, a four year old stallion The Irish Dragoon, and a home-bred mare, to display them at this prestigious Show. He and his helper, Pat Walsh, rode the two ponies to catch the train at Maam Cross, transferred them to the Dublin train at Galway station, rode them through Dublin to the docks, then loaded them on the boat to England, into trains again to London, and a repeat journey on the way back. The hardships of the journey took their toll and they had to cope with a very sick pony which had contracted tetanus on the return journey as a result of the confined travelling conditions.

The news of the long journey overland and by sea to London, stirred a new interest in the breed and the public debate which followed led eventually to the formation of a Breed Society some ten years later.

Chapter 5

The Connemara Pony Breeders Society

Chapter 5

When the Connemara Pony Breeders Society was established in 1923 by a group of concerned County Galway men, its members were to become the official guardians of the breed. They immediately took steps to restore the pony to its former, strong, hardy pre-famine native type by upgrading the breeding from within the existing herds. They decided to use only the best of the native stallions and mares to breed the traditional Connemara pony.

The First Connemara Pony Show

The dedicated Society members of the early nineteen twenties immediately began to plan a Connemara Pony Show to showcase the breed. The first Show took place in Roundstone in 1924 and this major Pony Show has run annually ever since. It changed venues in the early years but Clifden is now its permanent home.

A Stud Book was published in 1926 listing ponies, which on inspection, had been found to possess the desired characteristics of strength, hardiness, staying power, docility, intelligence and soundness. The breeding records have been regularly updated and nowadays you can trace the breeding of all registered Connemara ponies directly back to 1926 using the Society Stud Books.

Cannon Ball

Number One in that first Stud Book was a much respected and much used stallion, famous for his many racing wins. His name was Cannon Ball and he was descended from Welsh Cob and Native Connemara stock.

The imported Welsh Cob, the chestnut Prince Llewellyn, was the sire of Dynamite who was subsequently the sire of Cannon Ball. The dams of both Dynamite and Cannon Ball were native ponies.

Cannon Ball with owner Henri Toole

4

REGISTER OF STALLIONS.

No. 1.

CANNON BALL.

Foaled 1904. Colour : Grey. Marks : snip.
Height : 13 hands 3 inches.

Owner : Harry Toole, Leam, Oughterard.

No. 2.

CHARLIE.

Foaled 1922. Colour : Roan.
Height : 13 hands 2 inches.

Owner : Val Keaney, Gowla, Cashel.

No. 3.

CONNEMARA DAN.

Foaled 1922. Colour : Black, white star.
Height : 13 hands 1 inch.

Owner : James O'Toole, Faukeera, Clifden.

No. 4.

GALWAY GREY.

Foaled 1915. Colour : Grey. Marks : snip.
Height : 13 hands 3 inches.

Owner : Colman Conneely, Ballinahown, Galway.

No. 5.

GOLD DIGGER.

Foaled 1919. Colour : Dun, black points and small star.
Height : 13 hands 2 inches.

Owner : George Lyons, Bunakill, Maam Cross.

The first page of the first Connemara Pony Breeders Society Studbook

Faravane Boy by *May Boy-Farravane*

The Thoroughbred sire *Little Heaven* with Jack Bolger

Photo J. Walshe

Carna Dun, son of *Little Heaven-Double Dun* with Paddy Carr.

Outside Blood

Throughout the late nineteenth and early twentieth centuries, Thoroughbred blood was regularly used in parts of Connemara and the well known sires *Watchspring* and later *Thistleton* were often put to the native mare in order to produce fast racing ponies for the popular flapper races of that era. The resulting progeny were then entered in the Stud Book.

In subsequent years, in the forties and fifties, the Society again introduced outside blood, including Irish Draught, Thoroughbred and Arab. This was done to add substance and later, style and quality.

With the introduction of Draught blood such as that of *Skibbereen* and *May Boy* it was hoped to produce 'bone and power'and a heavier farm work-pony which would have a ready market in the agricultural south and east of the country. *Faravane Boy* was a son of *May Boy* and was sold to America to became No.1 in the American Society Studbook. *May Boy* stood firstly in Aran and then in Connemara for over ten years but by the middle of the century this market had dried up as mechanisation took over on farms and a lighter Riding Pony market was opening up, especially in Britain.

Among the out-crosses next used by the Society was a small bay Thoroughbred, *Little Heaven* who sired *Carna Dun* out of a Connemara mare called *Double Dun*.

Some of *Little Heaven*'s part-bred progeny who were to achieve major performance accolades included Dundrum who was the incredible small horse that show-jumped his way to world fame with Tommy Wade and was an International Jumping Champion from 1959 to 1963.

The Arab stallion *Naseel* sired *Clonkeehan Auratum* out of the Connemara mare *Western Lily* and both *Clonkeehan Auratum* and *Carna Dun* have made a prominent and lasting impression on the breed.

Although some limited Thoroughbred blood was again introduced in the 1970's, the Stud Book was closed to virtually all but offspring of registered stock by 1964.

Fortunately, and in spite of the influx of a variety of outside bloodlines, the average Connemara pony bred today has retained the characteristics of the original native breed. Because of the native mare prepotency — which is the power to breed true to themselves — and because native mares were always used, these qualities have remained with the breed, and are still dominant in the type of pony you will see today.

The Arab pony *Naseel*

Dundrum by *Carna Dun-Evergood*, with Tommy Wade in 1962

Clonkeehan Auratum by *Naseel-Western Lily:* Rider, author' 1956

Examples of the Connemara Pony family of today.

Yearling colt Nina's Boy by *Castlestrange Fionn-Dangan* Suzy with Bertie O'Halloran

Yearling filly by *Carraig Éibhir-Flaming Arrow* with Tomás MacLochlainn

Two year old filly, *Grange Anya Sparrow* by *Monaghanstown Fionn-Grange Agnes Sparrow*, with Padraic Heanue

Two year old colt *Fairyhill Gizmo* by *Castle Gizmo-Kingstown Fairy* with Rose Fitzgerald

Three year old mare *Glenkyle Cailín* by Glencarrig *Prince-Ballygarris Pretty Colleen* with Patrick Mahon

Mature mare *Castle Urchin* by *Abbeyleix Owen-Castle Dame* with Henry O'Toole

Mature stallion: Prolific Champion, *Glencarrig Prince* by *Cloonisle Cashel-Glencarrig Aedín* with Gearoid Curran

Filly foal by *Moy Hazy Cove* with dam *Mulbrey Breeze* with Michael Naughton

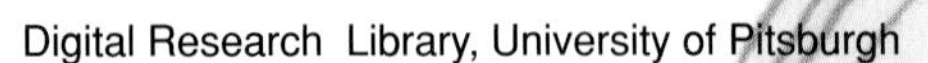
Digital Research Library, University of Pitsburgh

from The Mail Car, Jack B. Yeats.

Chapter 6

The changing role of the Connemara Pony

Aran work pony, mid twentieth century

Working pony, late nineteenth century

Chapter 6

Hard Working Ponies

The pony leads a very different life today to that of its forebear, the small farmer's workhorse, which was used for all the pulling and carting jobs needed throughout the farming year. With his owner, the pony did the ploughing, the tilling, sowing and reaping and the haymaking. Together they worked the small stony fields of Connemara, carting seaweed from the strands to enrich the small fields, where they grew corn, potatoes and other vegetables. They hauled stone from the quarries to construct roads and pulled turf from the bog to keep the family warm in winter and to cook the food at the open fire.

Only the strongest and bravest ponies survived this arduous and exhausting work as an animal who tired easily or whose temperament was 'faulty' was soon discarded by the farmer. The work-pony carried goods and family everywhere, to town or to markets many miles distant to sell farm produce, and carried family members to Mass, funerals and weddings all year round. The mare usually produced a foal each year, the sale of which brought much needed extra income into the household.

These working ponies often measured little more than 133 cms. in their studbook entry, and there was a greater number of blacks, browns, bays, duns and roans than the predominant grey of today's ponies.

Roan and Palomino, colours seldom seen today

Leisure Driving today: *Robe Thunder* by *Thunderball-Robe Mist* and *Glenadush Bertie* by *Derrigrah Robin-Calla* with David Morrison

Appearance today: Height, colour

The desired height of the breeding Connemara is normally 128 to 148 cms. inclusive. However the average height of the mature pony is currently 143 cms. to 153 cms., taller now than in former years, when the smaller, more wiry pony was the norm. In fact archaeologists have verified that Iron Age ponies of pre-Christian times, and even up to Medieval times, measured a maximum of 128 cms in height!

Eventing: *Tulira Katie Daly* by *New Beginnings-Tulira Mary Claire*, rider Sorcha North, owner Lady Anne Hemphill

Dressage: *Milford Sirocco* by *Milford Siskin-Mervyn Wren*, rider Shauna Finneran, owner M and R. Hardiman

Show-Jumping:*Ross Loobeen* by *Loobeen Larry-Glasson Lady*, rider Kyle Irvine, owner Kirstin McDonagh

Side-saddle: *Derrymore Paddy Finn* by *Cloonisle Cashel-Goodbye My Love* rider, Esme Mansergh-Wallace.

Working Hunter: Stallion, *Cashel Bay Prince* by *I Love You Melody-Coosheen Pheasant*, rider Claire Crawford, owner Robbie Fallon

Selective breeding and modern feeding has ensured that today's pony is a stronger animal with better conformation and movement and with more quality than the hard-worked, old fashioned forebear.

However, breeders have found that Connemara ponies that had survived for generations on a meagre diet of sparse grasses, reeds and herbs may grow too tall if fed soft, rich grass and hard feed, and 'pony character' may sometimes be lost. Some of todays young ponies may even look over-mature for their age. The genes of larger equines in the past, especially Arab, Thoroughbred and Draught, have also had an effect on the larger size and more robust appearance of the present day Connemara.

Colour

Grey is now the dominant pony colour of the pony, although most are born bay, brown, dun or black. The grey colour generally becomes whiter with age. Bays and duns are also popular at the moment, while the colours of black, palomino, cream, roan and chestnut are rarely seen now.

Versatile Breed

The modern Connemara Pony has become renowned as a performance pony, the ultimate all-rounder, capable of excelling in all equestrian sports. They feature in Pony Club and Riding Club activities, Showing, Show-jumping, Dressage, Cross-country and Eventing, Carriage Driving and Endurance Riding and will competently carry both child or adult in these sports.

Influential Breeds

Thoroughbred

Welsh Cob

Irish Draught

Arab pony

Throughout the development of the Connemara pony, breeders, including the Breeders Society, introduced a number of different breeds in an attempt to upgrade the native pony

Chapter 7

Learning to ride

Chapter 7

Buying a Connemara pony?

Owning a pony or two can be a marvellous experience for the entire family. However, before embarking on a buying expedition, reflect. Ask yourself whether you have the facilities, the interest and the commitment to keep a pony.

But first: Learn to ride before you buy!

As it would be unwise to even think of buying a Connemara pony before you acquire some experience of the skills needed to ride and care for it, riding lessons at a reputable riding school are advisable. Visit your riding centre beforehand and speak to a trained instructor. While you can also learn a lot from books, the hands-on experience and instruction are essential.

What to wear

You may think that what you wear is not important. However there is a reason for wearing the appropriate dress when learning to ride, and that is--SAFETY. You will need boots, either jodhpur or long boots, with a heel, to keep your feet from slipping through the stirrups. A professionally fitted and comfortable riding hat is of vital importance, while a back protector is also advisable. Jodhpurs or breeches are comfortable but stretch trousers will do. Riding gloves save your fingers from slipping or from being chafed by the reins. Your own riding stick is also essential. These last items are not expensive to buy.

Anna Murphy sensibly dressed to go riding.

Katelynn getting on board *Cú na Mara* by *Slisneoir-Mervyn Blue Tack*, held by Siobhán.

Swing the right leg over

Sit gently, straighten up and pat your pony.

Some relaxation exercises.
Stretch and bend

'Around the world'

Sample first lesson

Instructors will vary in their teaching methods, but a typical first riding lesson might be as follows:

Mounting

First make contact. Give your pony a rub on the neck while you let him have a look at you. As the instructor will stand at the pony's head you will be shown how to take the reins and some of the mane securely in your left hand, as you stand beside the pony at the pony's left side. Facing slightly to your right you will take the stirrup in your right hand and insert your left foot in the stirrup.

Getting on board

Now hold the reins and mane securely at the front (pommel) of the saddle with your left hand, making sure you don't pull the pony in the mouth. Stretch your right hand across to grip the skirt of the saddle on the far side. Push up with your right leg, swing the leg over, and lower yourself lightly into the saddle. Finally take up your reins in both hands held just above the pommel of the saddle, slip your feet into the stirrups, keeping the weight on the ball of your feet. The instructor will explain how to hold the reins.

Dismounting

Mounting will become automatic for you after a few sessions and a mounting block can also be used. To dismount, slide both feet out of the stirrups; with reins on the pommel with your left hand, swing your right leg back over the rump and land lightly on two feet.

Learning Basic Aids

Your instructor will walk you forward with a lead rope and you will get the feel of the pony's walk. You will learn to squeeze your legs on the pony's sides to move forward and you will learn to stop as well as start. You should keep your riding aids clear and simple as the pony has a fairly small brain and needs to understand what you are asking him. This first lesson will probably end with some trotting. Depending on progress, the first couple of lessons may be on the lead rein held by the instructor. You will now know the basic aids which are your hands, legs and the reins.

In the next couple of lessons you will be introduced to fun and games to accustom you to relax while you move around on your pony. Always have someone to hold the pony while you are practising the 'around the world' exercise.

Trotting on *Orwell*

The rising trot and moving on

Your pony may wear a neck strap which you will be asked to hold on to and a neck strap is helpful in establishing balance and rhythm in the rising trot. After watching another rider demonstrate the rising trot, you will get the idea of rhythm with the trotting movement.

As your pony follows another around the school or arena in trot, you will be able to concentrate on your own riding aids and on keeping your hands quiet and low on the reins and neck strap. After a few sessions you will find that you yourself are doing a satisfactory rising trot. Always try to land lightly in the saddle on the sitting part to avoid bumping the pony's back.

Mucking out

Sweepng up

Alana wonders where to start!

Siobhán shows Katelyn how to put the bridle together

Cantering and games

Soon the typical routine in lessons will involve bending through cones, trotting over poles and going over a small jump. Learning to sit to a canter will come easily as it will usually be a 'follow the leader' session. By the end of a few more lessons you will be proficient in walk, trot and canter and will understand a lot more of the 'pony-mentality' and characteristics than you did before starting to ride.

Learning 'the groom's' work

Learning to ride and control your mount effectively and to become an accomplished rider, takes quite some time to master. Meanwhile, spending time at the riding centre will be invaluable especially when you are allowed to watch and to help out. You will learn some basic stable management such as feeding and caring for the animals and you may be surprised to learn that so much work is involved. Leather saddles and bridles must be regularly cleaned and oiled to keep them safe and supple It will not take long to discover that it's not all about just sitting up on the animal and 'hey-ho off we go'!

Riding Camps

Riding Schools will sometimes run a five day camp with varied activities which are fun for their pupils, usually during the school holidays. Here you can also pick up plenty of extra information as well as getting the opportunity of riding experience twice each day.

Chapter 8

The Pony Club

'Minders', Pony Club junior members at Errislannon Pony Club Junior Camp

Learning about hay and feed

Rugs and how to use them

Chapter 8

Children from about seven years of age or over are advised to join a local branch of the Pony Club if possible, and here you will come by most of the necessary skills involved in caring for and riding a pony. Pony Clubs also run residential camps which involve total immersion in a pony world, usually for a five day week, dealing with all aspects of riding and pony care.

The aims of the Irish Pony Club are as follows; **A. To encourage young people to ride and to learn to enjoy all kinds of sport connected with horses and riding. B. To provide instruction in riding and horsemanship, and to instill in members the proper care of their animals. C. To promote the highest ideals of sportsmanship, citizenship and loyalty, thereby cultivating strength of character and self-discipline.**

You don't have to have your own pony to join the Pony Club and you can sometimes hire one from the riding school. You will be helped and encouraged to turn yourself and your pony out in top condition at all times.

Learning and Doing

As well as riding lessons you will learn stable management. The daily agenda will include practice at keeping your pony and the stable clean and learning the basics of feeding, as well as recognising the different types of feed. You will learn to tack up and untack, and to care for saddles, bridles and other necessary equipment.

Tips on watering, grooming and rugging-up are also included. You will learn how to handle ponies of varying moods and habits, and you will learn through practical demonstrations, plus lectures and videos, that there is a safe way as well as an unsafe way to work with ponies and horses.

You should learn about necessary care of the feet and the work of the farrier, as well as the need to worm your pony on a regular basis.

Farrier Shane Carey at work on *Fred Astaire* by *Monaghanstown Fred*

Sandra O'Donnell loads *Clough Colleen* by *Clough Joey-Lady Tara*, slowly and safely

Learning the stepping stones game

Teaching and learning

Trotting poles

Pony Club Hunter Trials

Learning how to load and unload the pony into and out of a trailer and to ride out safely is also a necessary part of Pony Club instruction.

Activities

Mounted games, jumping and dressage are usually part of the camp activities and some Pony Clubs will have extra facilities where you can also try your skill at cross-country or polo. You can study for any number of badges, all the time adding to your equestrian skills.

Usually you will work and ride with like-minded 'horsey kids' so there is a strong fun element attached! There are organised outings to other Pony Club branches where games, jumping, dressage and hunter trials may be run as well as Tetrathlon events involving running, shooting and swimming, as well as cross-country riding for more experienced members.

These activities and skills are all part of the sport you have chosen and a Pony Club experience will stand to you no matter what you decide to do with the pony you eventually buy.

Riding Clubs

For those enthusiasts in a slightly older age group it is worth joining a Riding Club in your Area. **The Association of Irish Riding Clubs aims to 'encourage riding as a sport and recreation, to promote good fellowship among riders and to improve and maintain the standard of riding and horsemastership in Ireland.'**

They have over 121 affiliated Clubs nationwide; the sole requirement is that you must be 17 years of age or over and you don't even have to own a horse to be involved. Some Clubs are more competitive while others will have a greater social slant. Fun for both rider and horse or pony is the main constituent of these Riding Clubs.

Chapter 9

Purchasing a Connemara Pony

It has come to the stage where you badly want your own pony, you have made the decision and you are wondering where to look and what to look for. If you have been riding regularly for at least a year you will now be ready for this experience.

Looking: Breeders, Shows, Sales, Inspections.

The Connemara area itself has many breeders, usually with stock to sell, and there are many other breeders countrywide and abroad. A current list of breeders can be obtained from the Breeders Society Office in Clifden. It is a good idea to look out for Connemara classes at Shows around the country, to develop an eye for the good type of pony. All ponies, like people, are slightly different but some have better conformation than others and mares may have a different shape than colts or geldings.

Family favourite at Claddaghduff Show

Shows

During the Summer, from May to September, practically every weekend will have a Connemara Pony Show or an Agricultural Show running somewhere in the West of Ireland, and indeed throughout the entire country. In Connemara itself the emphasis is on the pony showing in-hand with a number of ridden classes, usually towards the end of the day. Classes are held for ponies in all age groups from foals, young fillies and colts, to stallions, geldings, and mares of every age, with Championships at the end of the Junior and the Senior sections. These Connemara Pony Shows are a major social event and a great atmosphere of camaraderie and friendship prevails among the many small breeders who show their animals.

The stallion *Currachmore Cashel* by *Rosenharley Rowley-Tolka Bridge*, trotted up by Eamon Burke at Clifden Show

There will usually be a dog show, classes for sheep, home produce competitions, arts and crafts, food wagons, inflatables and carnival rides for children and with Irish dancing and music thrown in, the whole affair, on a bright sunny day, can be a most enjoyable experience.

A busy mare and foal class at Ballyconneely Show

Prizewinning mare, *Coosheen Pheasant* by *Callowfeenish Mairtín-Coosheen Swallow*, with owners Robbie and Barbara Fallon.

Loughmore McDara Óg, 2yr old colt by *Ormond Oliver-Corrib Misty* with Mossie Joyce at Claregalway Show

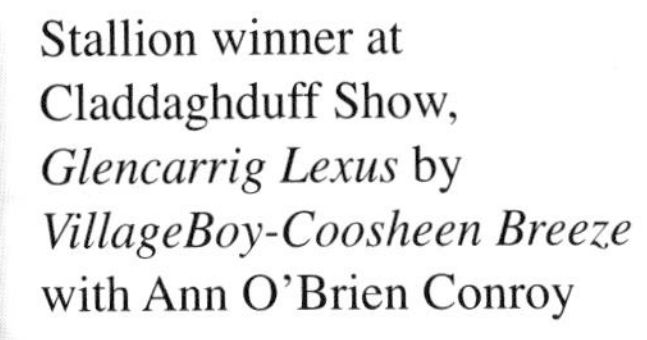

Stallion winner at Claddaghduff Show, *Glencarrig Lexus* by *VillageBoy-Coosheen Breeze* with Ann O'Brien Conroy

Coosheen Breeze by *Coosheen Finn-Scarteen Minstral* winning the older mares class at Oughterard Show at age 19, with Ciaran Curran.

Sales

Attending Connemara Pony Sales can also be a helpful and worth-while experience, except that you may be unprepared for - or be flummoxed by - the sometimes chaotic sight of so many foals and young ponies being offered for sale together.

Inspections

If there is an Inspection Day of young ponies near you, visit and take note. These take place at various venues around the country each Spring, Here you will see young-stock being checked by an inspection team who will award marks for type, conformation and movement. The ponies will then be measured, marked and microchipped by a vet, before their owners can apply for the Connemara Pony passport.

Viewing

Decide what you wish to do with this pony that will soon be yours and look out for the pony that will best serve your needs. For instance, you may wish to purchase a Connemara mare for breeding, or you may be looking for a schoolmaster-type mare or gelding who has done everything and knows the 'riding ropes'.

A younger type may appeal, as it is most satisfying to bring on and produce a youngster provided you have the necessary experience. Training and backing is not usually done until the pony is 3 – 4 years old and considered developed and strong enough for work with a rider. Unless you are very experienced it is better if a professional trainer prepares a young pony for backing and riding. This will involve patient lungeing and long-reining before the saddle is introduced. There will still be plenty of schooling work for you to do as a young pony will do a lot of

At the Sales, Clifden Mart

Line-up in Connemara Ridden Class, riders under 16, at Westport Show

Tom Lydon long-reins *'Colonel'*, or *Clough Ross* by *Ross Castle Fred-Gortnalea Smokie*

A family checking out *Mo Chara Fionn* by *Castlestrange Fionn-Cití*, at Spiddal Show, with John M. Mulligan

learning before it is fully trained and riding forward in a balanced, free and obedient manner. Don't forget to make sure your chosen Connemara is registered with the Breeders Society, or is eligible for registration, and that the transfer of ownership is then recorded with the Society.

When the time comes to arrange to view a pony, it is best to bring a knowledgeable person along who will advise you. Whatever you wish to purchase, be mindful of the need for good temperament, good conformation and the 'docility, intelligence and soundness' recommended by the founders of the Breeders Society all those years ago.

Keeping in mind that some things never change, read over the guidelines devised by the Breeders Society.

Chapter 10

THE CONNEMARA PONY BREEDERS SOCIETY, GUIDELINES

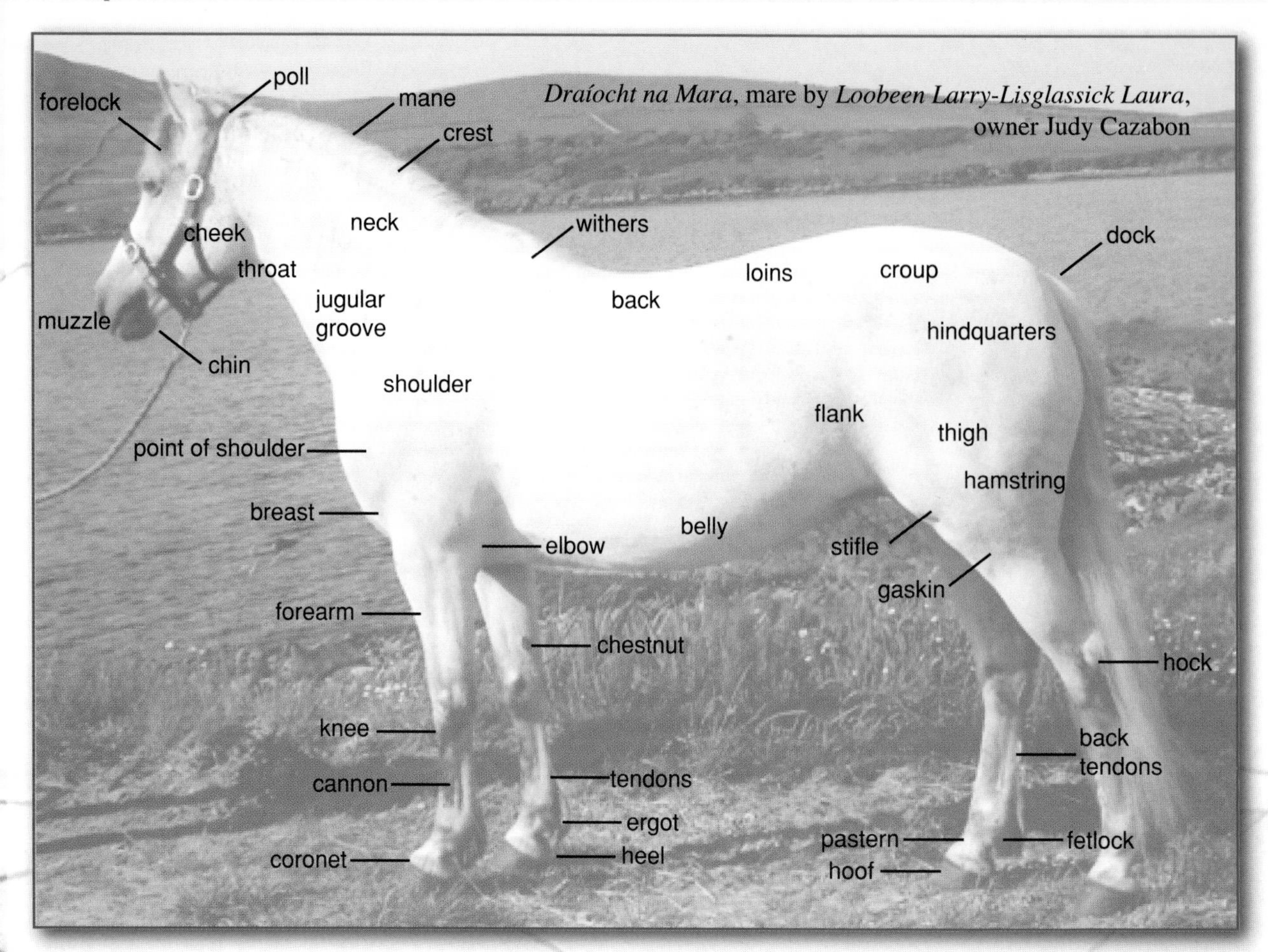

1 Head
Well balanced pony head of medium length with good width between large kindly eyes. Pony ears, well defined cheekbone, jaw relatively deep but not coarse.

2 Front
Head well set onto neck. Crest should not be over developed. Neck not set on too low. Good length of rein. Well defined withers, good sloping shoulders.

3 Body
Body should be deep, with strong back, some length permissible but should be well ribbed up and with strong loins

4 Limbs
Good length and strength in forearm, well defined knees and short cannons, with flat bone measuring 18cms.to 21cms Elbows should be free. Pasterns of medium length, feet well shaped, of medium size, hard and level.

Gentle Wren, mare (head and neck) by *Abbeyleix Owen-Milford Wren*, owner John McLoughlin

Glencarrig Princess, 4yr old by *Glencarrig Prince-Belmont Lady,* owner Lady Vestey

Kingstown Molly 2nd by *Coral Prince-Kingstown Molly*, and her 11 day old filly foal, owner John Noel Mullen

5 Hind quarters
Strong and muscular with some length, well developed second thighs (Gaskin) and strong low-set hocks

6 Movement
Movement free, easy and true, without undue knee action, but active and covering the ground.

A closer look

If you pause to think about these guidelines it will become obvious why the Breed Society looks for the type of conformation specified above, bearing in mind that a pony of poor conformation will be more prone to disease and injury.

Points 1 and 2, **Head and Front** speak for themselves as a beautiful head and neck is 'easy on the eye' because it is part of the balanced look of the animal. The shape of the neck will also affect head carriage and a good sloping shoulder will give a more comfortable ride and better movement.

Point 3, Body. A deep girth and a broad front ensure good space for lungs and heart. A narrow front may mean having the two front legs too close together to allow for good straight movement. The body may be longer in a mare to allow for carrying a foal.

Point 4, limbs, sets out the guidelines for good limbs. It means that you should always check that the legs are straight when viewed from the front and back and that there is 'good bone'. Bone is measured as the width around the leg directly below the knee. Sloping pasterns act as a buffer against concussion.

Point 5, Hind quarters. Look at the limbs from the side and the back. Hocks should not turn in behind (cow-hocks) and the hooves should have no marked rings or grooves.

Point 6, Movement. Look for straight movement as the pony is trotted toward you.

Kingstown Fionn, stallion by *Monaghanstown Fionn-Kingstown Silver*, owner Malachy Gorham

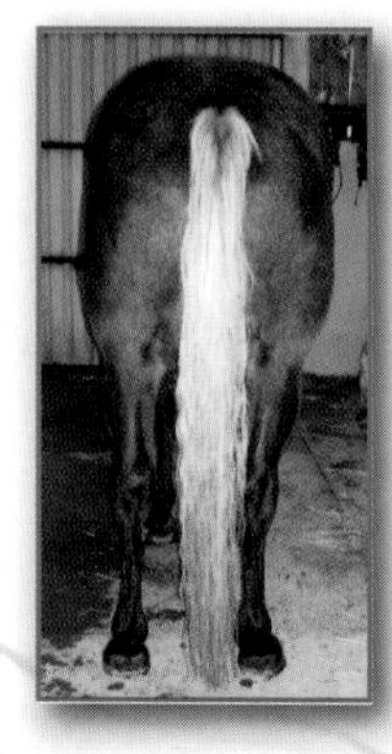

Hind quarters and back legs, *Kingstown Fionn*

Milford Sirocco, gelding, is trotted up by Shauna

Castle Squire, Stallion by *Abbeyleix Owen-Village Star*, owner John Varley

Aran Andy by *Ardravinna Andy-Aran Melissa* with Siobhán Cazabon-Sullivan

Salerna-Sunset by *Abbeyleix Owen-Munga Mary Ann,* rider Kathryn Byrne

Overall a well-balanced look is the one you are looking for.

Having looked at your pony in hand, you can ask for a ridden pony to be ridden. Watch it at walk, trot and canter and if the pony has jumped ask to see it jumping. Note the attitude and 'way of going' for his rider before you try it out yourself.

It is also helpful to see the pony in the field and stable and to see how it responds to the owner's handling.

Sometimes an owner does not mind a prospective buyer taking the pony home on a week's trial to see if pony and rider are suited, and it is worth asking if this is possible. However don't be surprised if you receive a polite refusal as many owners have been badly burned by this move in the past.

Finally you may arrange for the pony to be 'vetted', that is, given a thorough examination by a vet of your choice.

Chapter 11

Maintenance, Field and Stable

Chapter 11

During your Connemara pony-search you will need to look into all the necessities of life which your new pony is going to need. First of all, the pony's home is very important. An environment suitable for equines is not always easy to find unless you already have some land to call your own or a rentable alternative

Fenced paddocks and company, with trees providing natural shelter

The Field: Benefits of grass

All horse owners know the value of keeping their animal out on grass as much as possible. Grass contains essential nutrients and a long period daily out in a field and especially a complete break annually, out on grass, will make all the difference to your pony's mental and physical health. This will give him an opportunity to get back to nature, to graze and wander as he wishes, to kick up his heels and have a good gallop, or to roll in the mud and engage in some mutual grooming with a companion, while ridding himself of stable- induced frustrations

Winter and Summer Grazing

The ideal home would have a ready supply of grazing, winter as well as summer, with natural or man-made shelter. However, winter grazing can be a rarity in Ireland, especially in Connemara, and grass nutrients may be low, so winter feeding with hay is necessary. If your grazing area does not have natural shelter, ie. hilly land, trees, hedges or high walls you will need some form of three-sided shelter with a wide entrance so that your pony may escape from the winter rain and wind or the summer flies. Fencing must be strong and durable and the pony must have a constant fresh water supply and a mineral lick in a bucket. Unless there is access to a stream of clean running water you will need to break the ice each day on top of water containers in icy winter weather.

Mares and foals, good company

Young stock mature together

Farriers at work

Avoid overgrazing and poisonous plants

You should have enough land (1 – 2 acres per pony) to close off paddocks to avoid overgrazing and poaching in winter when land can become 'horse sick' and take months to recover. It is handy also to be able to fence off areas with electric fencing and so restrict your pony's grazing when the grass becomes lush and plentiful in the Spring. Keep an eye out then for poisonous plants such as ragwort and pull them out by the roots and burn early in the growing season, to prevent the spread of the weed

A field companion

Bear in mind that the Connemara pony, in common with all equines, is a herd animal and will not be contented if left alone in a field without company. If another equine is not available, then sheep, cattle or a pair of goats may be introduced. The ideal solution to droppings is to clear them daily, and if you are lucky enough to own one, a quad and a special hoover attachment is the most effective way. Field gates that are easy for you to open and close make life easier. The last thing you need is to have a second pony running out of your field as you try to lead out number one and close a sticky gate on pony number two at the same time!

The Stable

Your Connemara will need to be housed occasionally, particularly in winter and especially if you are planning to show the pony or to compete in any equestrian sport.

Your vet and farrier will need to treat or shoe your animal under cover, especially in inclement weather conditions.

A well-ventilated stable, with slightly sloping floor for drainage, fitted with an automatic drinker or freshly filled water bucket, is recommended A tying ring for a hay-net, or to tie up your pony, is a necessity and make sure the stable has no sharp edges. If you use the comfortable rubber matting you will still need bedding to soak up wetness.

Company

A stable companion helps to keep boredom and loneliness at bay, as the stable is not a natural environment for the Connemara pony although most adapt well.

Storage and stable bedding

You will also need adequate storage to keep your tack, feed and hay and bedding secure, dry and free from vermin. A resident family cat can be a useful addition here. Bedding, either straw, wood shavings which you can buy in bales, or finely shredded paper, are all good bedding materials if they are dust-free. Heap the bedding up at the sides to help avoid the pony getting cast and keep it deep in the centre. Getting cast in the stable means that when rolling or lying down he may get stuck on his back too close to the wall to right himself again without a major struggle.

Stable cleaning equipment,

The stabled pony will need the stable mucked out, or droppings removed, daily. If you use shavings, a shavings fork is a must; for straw a four pronged fork is a good mucking out tool. A wheelbarrow, a shovel and a yard-brush are also essential You can never have too many buckets or other suitable containers which you will use for water, for feeding, and for washing your pony.

Stables

Hay, feed and bedding will need to be kept in a covered, secure area

A stable well banked-up with straw

Some mucking-out tools and fresh straw

A high-fibre, low-sugar feed

Ponies really love healthy carrots and apples

Feeding

Good grass, or good clean, quality hay or haylage, plus a mineral lick is the only food needed when the pony is not in work. When stabled, fresh water and hay should be available ad lib to mimic the natural grazing instinct.

Feeding for work

If he is working most days, that is, being schooled, jumping, hunting or doing fast work he will need extra energy-giving food. Some Connemaras, like all ponies, will get a little too 'sharp' if fed heating mixes, so go easy on the high sugar content feeds or better still,avoid them. Look for a high-fibre content instead. Feed companies now produce a wide variety of mixed grains, rather than the pony nuts, bran, oats, barley and beet pulp of former years, so it is easier to find fibre-rich, low-sugar feeds today. Feed according to the maker's instructions and you will quickly learn to vary this to suit your pony's temperament.

If feeding hard feed, ie pony nuts or a pony mix, allow sufficient time, an hour at least, for your pony to digest the feed before tacking up and exercising him. Use feed bins to keep out mice or worse!; these can be ordinary bins of metal or heavy plastic with secure lids.

The ideal is to feed 'little and often'. Feed carrots and apples also, especially when grass is not growing. Never feed freshly saved hay, it should be allowed to season for at least two months before being fed to your pony. Oil, either boiled linseed or cod liver oil, or cooking oil from the kitchen, can be added to the feed. This is good for joints and will also give a special sheen to the coat.

Chapter 12

Grooming and Basic Tack

Grooming kit

Picking out the feet

- Dandy brush
- Curry comb
- Rubber curry comb (for dry mud removal)
- Body brushes
- Sponges
- Sweat scraper
- Mane combs
- Hoof picks and Scissors
- Hoof oil and brush
- Cloth rubber

This is the basic grooming kit to which you can add a myriad of other useful items that you will find in tack shops.

Grazing in Winter

A 'thatched' pony drying out

Always tie up your pony with a quick release knot before starting to groom and always pick out the feet first, shod or unshod. Teach your pony good manners in and out of the stable. He must not be allowed to rush in or out, and should learn to move sideways when given a slight shove and of course should stand quietly for grooming. Be quiet and calm but firm, at all times, with your Connemara.

Winter

The Connemara pony grows a fine warm winter coat, yet the pony will love to roll in the muddiest part of the field, and this serves a very useful purpose, as the dried mud will prevent heat loss through the skin, a little like your thermal vest in the way it retains body heat. The result of a mud bath is not a pretty sight but a hay or straw wisp, which you can make yourself, is the best way to remove dried field mud from the coat before using any brushes. The rubber curry comb is also useful for this. Do not over-use the dandy brush as the natural grease in the skin is also needed for insulation purposes outdoors.

As long as the saddle, bridle and girth areas are dry and clean the pony can be saddled up and ridden. If your pony is wet and is going to be ridden, rub him briskly with a wisp to help warm him up and be especially careful to clean the girth area as a pony with an itchy tummy will not be slow to show his displeasure!

'Thatching' is also a good way to dry off a cold wet pony This means a coat of straw or hay is made by laying the 'thatch' under a light rug, kept in place by a surcingle, and allowing the pony to warm up and dry at the same time. A sweat-rug can be a useful item too.

A Connemara pony does not actually need a New Zealand outdoor rug unless you wish to work him, as in jumping in a Winter League, or taking him hunting. For this he will need a partial clip to avoid sweating up and getting cold afterwards and then he will need to be rugged. You will also need a stable rug and a light travel rug as well as travel boots and tail protection.

Grooming in Summer

Summer

A daily grooming is needed for the part-stabled pony. With the field- kept pony, only groom when completely dry. With a dandy brush, lightly brush along the natural line of the coat to remove any dried mud. With the body brush, do likewise, but lean on the body brush and clean after every few strokes with the curry- comb held in your other hand. Use a smaller brush to gently brush the face and head around the ears. Brush through the tail, holding it bit by bit to avoid breaking hairs. Only brush out the tail fully when you are preparing to bring the pony somewhere, like a Show or a Pony Club Rally or some such event, as brushing out each time you groom would pull hairs out and eventually leave a rather thin tail.

Basic tack

The very minimum you need are as follows:

- Simple snaffle bridle
- General purpose saddle
- Two girths, one for Shows or as a spare
- Headcollars
- Lead ropes
- Neck strap or spare stirrup leather

Essential tack: saddle with stirrups and girth, bridle with bit, headcollars and lead ropes

Tack neatly stored

Rebecca saddle-soaping some tack

Bits: There are a number of different types of snaffle bits, some with single or double-jointed mouthpiece, some with loose rings or fixed rings known as egg-butt snaffles. In pony magazines and in tack shops you will see a huge variety of bits, bridles and other equipment, but again ask your instructor's advice. It is advisable that you and your new pony will continue to go for help, lessons and advice for some time.

There are special **saddles** made for dressage, show-jumping and showing but a well fitting general-purpose saddle, of a reputable brand, is a good first buy.

Cleaning Tack

The saddle

The saddle should have stirrup leathers removed for cleaning and the stirrups should be washed or wiped with a damp cloth before use, to supple it up. It should be kept clean and well-oiled if you want it to last.

The girth, stirrup irons and stirrup leathers are bought separately when you are buying the saddle. All new leather will need saddle soap, cream, or leather dressing before use to supple it up and will need to be kept clean and well oiled if you want it to last.

The bridle

You should regularly take your leather tack apart for cleaning. Make sure to check the positions of your bridle straps and buckles before the dismantling operation, or you are going to have some fun putting it all together correctly! The bit should be rinsed out under a hot tap after use. Never use ordinary soap or wash-up liquid on your tack, only saddle soap or oil.

Chapter 13

Preparing for a Show

Washing

As most Connemaras are grey, bath-time is an essential part of any Show preparation, and often provides the lucky owner with a free bath too!

The ideal pony-washing day is warm and sunny with a fresh breeze, so that the pony will not get cold while being washed and will dry quickly. You will need a bucket of warm soapy water, large sponges and a brush to scrub the mane and body. To get a pristine white look to body, mane and tail, some old fashioned 'blue bag' in the washing water is a good idea. You can also buy a mild modern laundry bleaching product, but try it out first on a small area of skin.

Do not use these cleaners on a non-white Connemara or you may end up with a peculiar looking pony! You can also buy mane and tail conditioner which will give a soft and shining texture after washing. Rinse him off well, using a water hose pipe. Scrape off excess water with a sweat-scraper, and walk him around until nearly dry. A sweat rug will help with the drying if the sunshine is not doing the job.

Eavan starts washing *Dangan Rose* by *Coosheen Bailey-Dangan Molly*

Ruth rinses the tail

The mane and tail

After untangling if necessary and brushing, use a damp water brush to lay the mane. Use your fingers to separate tail hairs and lightly brush through. It is usual for Connemaras to be shown with full manes and tails as they are native ponies. However you will need to lightly thin, and tidy the mane and pull straggly hairs, from the roots, as you go along. The mane will probably need to be plaited if you are entered in non-Connemara pony classes.

Connemara mane

Trimming jaw hairs

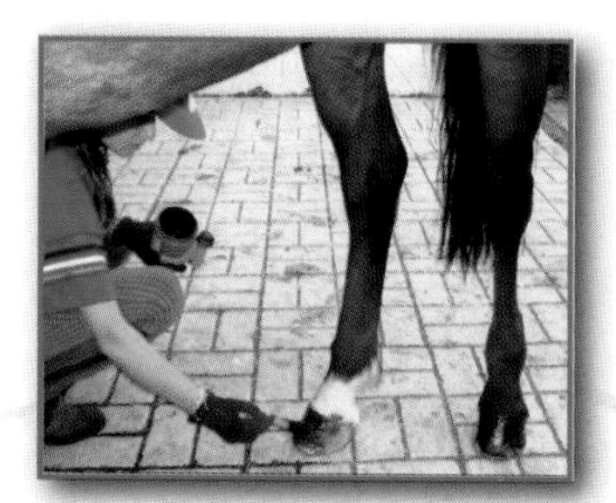

Applying hoof oil

Connemara tail

The Connemara tail is best shining-clean, long and flowing but can be very lightly tidied at both sides at the top to give a neater look. Wash face and forelock very carefully and gently, with a damp lukewarm sponge. Use separate damp sponges to sponge eyes, nostrils and dock. Trim along the outside of the ears only and along the jaw line to give a cleaner look. Leave feather on the fetlocks but tidy the back of the pasterns and round the hooves. You can finish off with hoof oil for a really smart look, but carefully, to avoid smudging oil on the freshly washed legs.

Before competing at a Show

If you decide to show your Connemara In-Hand, practice at home by getting the pony to walk out and trot well with you at his shoulder and to stand square and still when required. Schooling and getting your pony fit at home for whatever you will be doing is essential; whether in Ridden Classes or perhaps competing in Working Hunter Classes or Show-jumping, or Dressage.

Try in advance to get him used to unusual sights and sounds, such as loud music, noisy tractors, umbrellas, or tents and lorries, and above all, have him in very obedient mode. Some people will even go so far as to hang up balloons and flapping bunting in view of the field or stable. You never know what may startle him at a busy bustling agricultural show!

Umbrella going up!

If this is new to both of you, then perhaps bring the pony along to a Show in a trailer first and show him the sights or ride him around without actually entering any competitions. Take note of tack and dress in different competitions. On show day make sure to arrive well before your class or competition to allow time for collecting numbers, riding him in, and making sure that you haven't forgotten anything. If you have you will then still have time to borrow.

Dangan Rose is plaited for a good Working Hunter turnout for rider Eavan Murphy

The main ingredient

If you do get involved in the Showing scene however, there are some things that can not be borrowed: so make sure to take with you both a sense of humour and a good dollop of patience, as Shows can be testing as well as being fun!

A box containing a basic grooming kit is useful. A pony travel rug, travel boots and a tail bandage will complete the ensemble. You will also need a haynet, a water container, feed, buckets for food and water and sponges for working on new stains acquired during travel. You will of course have remembered to pack the pony's saddle and bridle, if you are planning to ride!

Naoise and *Aran Andy* with some necessities for the day

Shown In-Hand by Henry O'Toole, *Janus,* stallion, by *Oxenholm Marble-Brants Hamme*r *Julie*.

A tail bandage protects the tail during travel. Esmé is dressed for the Ring

Showing a pony in-hand

Your Connemara pony should have learned to show in hand, walking and trotting-out well with the handler walking clockwise at his shoulder, to allow the judges an uninterrupted view of the animal. Have the pony used to standing square and still, and moving off at your request. Pony and handler must be clean and neatly turned out. When turning the pony in walk in order to trot back towards the judge, always make a clockwise turn to ensure the judges get a full-on view of the pony and not the handler.

Riding the pony

The rider will be neatly dressed with clean jodhpurs, shirt and tie or stock, hat and boots, riding jacket, gloves, your stick or showing cane and tape or bootlace to tie on your number around your waist. Girls should not forget a hairnet and hair tie and omit the jewellery! All the small, fiddly bits are best kept permanently together in one container.

Finally, but most necessary, is the presence of your helper, driver, groom and general 'gofor' A well filled picnic bag is also a good idea and a real bonus for the humans involved.

Chapter 14

Health and Well-being

Foot care

Your Connemara pony will need to be shod unless he is going to spend all his time on grass or on a sand surface. His feet, shod or unshod, will need regular paring and trimming by the farrier. Shoes are necessary to protect the feet if he is working on any hard surface or is ridden on the road. It is the farrier's job to keep your pony's feet in good condition and to fit him with the correct size and shape of shoe. The pony will need new shoes on average every six to eight weeks or if the shoes are not worn down, he can have 'removes', ie feet trimmed and the same shoes replaced. Oil the feet inside and outside regularly to prevent dryness and cracking.

Clough Colleen being attended to by farrier Cecil Fitzgerald, for Tom Lydon

Marking, measuring, 'chipping' and vaccinations

If you wish to take part in affiliated competitions, such as. Showjumping or Irish Pony Society showing and jumping Classes, the pony will need to be marked and measured by a vet at a recognised measuring centre, usually a riding school. The information gained will subsequently be added to the Connemara passport. Nowadays, when all horses and ponies are obliged to have a passport, the microchip number will also be added. These official measuring and marking sessions are regularly held in late Winter/early Spring, and ponies need to have four such measurings between the ages of four and eight years.

Your vet should be contacted about the necessity of 'flu and tetanus vaccinations if you are going to compete seriously. Many stable yards will not admit horses or ponies without the necessary vaccinations stamped on the passport.

Vet giving 'flu and tetanus vaccination to the stallion *Silver Shadow* by *Cloonisle Cashel-Poetic Moonlight*

Vet Philip and John prepare to rasp the pony's teeth

Teeth care

Teeth should be checked by the vet at least once a year, and more often if there is a problem with the pony accepting the bit, as sharp teeth or wolf teeth, which some ponies have, may be painful and cause problems when the pony is ridden.

Teeth may need rasping or wolf teeth may need to be removed, and this is a simple and routine treatment. Fortunately Connemara ponies are usually much calmer than people about visiting the dentist!

Worming

Regular worming every few months will be necessary and this you can do yourself using the special syringe paste-wormers for equines. If you happen to buy-in an animal whose worming history may be dubious, your vet will do a tubing procedure which is a very effective worming practice.

Siobhán worming pony

A special satisfaction

If you think that owning a Connemara pony sounds like an enormous amount of work, take heart. The care of your pony and your attention to his health, psychological as well as physical, will pay dividends. The result will be a happy, well adjusted and biddable animal and this will bring you, his minder, a special satisfaction. Children will soon learn to become responsible and reliable carers, and will happily give their pony undivided attention every day of the year. Connemara pony ownership will develop the age old bond between the animal, the land and people. It will add an unrivalled and pleasurable dimension to your life.

Aideen with *Maodhóg of Ards* by *Holiday Archfield-Lady Penelope*

APPENDIX

Other Equine activities

You will now be interested in finding out more about the many activities you and your Connemara pony can do together. There is of course simple hacking or trekking out with friends. If you wish to try more activities, the most common and most accessible sports you can choose from are Showing, including ridden and jumping classes for Connemara ponies, Show-jumping, Hunter Trials, Dressage, Eventing, Pony Club activities, Riding Clubs, Endurance or Long Distance Riding, Polo or Polocross, Driving and Hunting.

There are organisations which promote each of these disciplines, and a phone call to any of these will give you all the information you may require to get involved in their sport.

Connemara Pony Breeders Society
The Showgrounds, Clifden, Connemara
Co. Galway
Tel: 095 21863
Fax: 095 21005
www.cpbs.ie

International Committee of Connemara Pony Societies
Secretariat, Mrs. Susan Rinehart
1085 Wood Lane, Charlottesville
VA 22901-5038, USA
Tel: 434-295 7777
Fax: 434-295 0366
Email: susanrinehart@mindspring.com.

The Irish Pony Club
Tinnascarty, Freshford, Co. Kilkenny
Tel: 056-8832966
Fax: 056 8832965
www.irishponyclub.ie

Show Jumping Association of Ireland
Kildare Paddocks, Kill, Co. Kildare
Tel: 045 842300
Fax: 045 842301
www.sjai.ie

Irish Pony Society
ITBA House, Greenhills, Kill, Co. Kildare
Tel: 045 878987
Fax: 045 878871
www.irishponysociety.ie

Association of Irish Riding Clubs
Waverly House, Church Road
Greystones, Co. Wicklow
Tel: 0818 - 270227
Fax: 01-2010781
www.airc.ie

Dressage Ireland Ltd.
Dove House, Killedmond
Borris, Co. Carlow
Tel 059 9771728
Fax: 059 9771728
www.dressageireland.ie

Eventing Ireland
Kildare Paddocks, Kill, Co. Kildare
Tel: 045 886674
Fax: 045 886675
www.eventingireland.com

Side-Saddle Association of Ireland
Mulberry Manor Farm
Rathbeggan, Dunshaughlin, Co. Meath
Tel: 01-8241762
Fax: 01-8241674

Irish Long Distance Riding Association
138 Navanfort Road, Armagh
Co Armagh
BT60 4PX
Tel: 02837-524809
Fax: 02837-524809
www. Ildra.co.uk

Carriage Driving Ireland
Ballybane House, Nangor Road,
Clondalkin, Dublin 22
Tel: 086-3043154.

Riding for the Disabled Association Ireland
Rathlinn, Templecarrig Lower,
Delgany, Co. Wicklow.
Tel: 01-2876498
Fax: 01-2876503
www.rdai.org

The Photo Album

Cannon Ball 1 by *Dynamite, Welsh Cob-Connemara Cross*, foaled 1904: with owner Henri Toole

The Photo Album is made up of a representative sample of Connemara ponies, mainly of times past. The captions contain the Connemara Pony Breeders Stud Book number, names of the Sire and Dam and the name of the breeder, owner and rider when available.

Some ponies were noted Show Ring winners. Others, both stallions and mares, produced champions in a variety of equestrian disciplines. All of the ponies, including geldings, have contributed to the reputation of the quality Connemara Pony we know today.

An effort has also been made to include as many bloodlines as possible.

Unfortunately, because of space restrictions, many more good ponies of the past and present are not included in this Gallery.

Rebel 7 by *Cannon Ball* foaled 1922: with owner Val Keaney

Carna Bobby 79 by *Gil-Carna Dolly*, foaled 1946: breeder Patrick Mulkerrin: with B.J. Bermingham

Noble Star 17 by *Black Paddy* foaled 1928: owner Ml. J. O'Neill, with Jack Bolger

Carna Dun 89 by *Little Heaven T.B – Double Dun*, foaled 1948, breeder John Mylotte: with Paddy Carr Photo Jimmy Walshe

Silver Pearl 18 by *John Quirke-Bess*, foaled 1931: owner Stephen Walsh, with Jack Bolger

Photo Station House Museum, Clifden

MacDara 91 by *Dun Lorenzo-Dolan Rose*, foaled 1949, breeder John McCahill

Gill 43 by *Inchagoill Laddie-Golden Gleam*, foaled 1938: with John Walsh

Inver Rebel 93 by *Lavelly Rebel-Inver Bridge*, foaled 1950, breeder Pat Mulkern: with Martin Walsh in 1960

Bridge Boy 124 by *Tooreen Ross-Irene,* foaled 1959, owner Paddy Geoghegan

Kimble 227 by *Dun Aengus-Inver Colleen*, foaled 1965, breeder Christie Lydon: with owner Willie Diamond

Lambay Rebel 131 by *MacDara-Moonshine*, foaled in 1960, breeder Martin Gorham: with Michael O'Connell,

Finn Mac Cool 228 by *Camlin Cicada-Fionnog*, foaled 1965, with Michael O'Connell

Little Joe 165 by *Carna Dun-Cregg Lassie*, foaled 1963, breeder James Walsh: with owner John Stagg.

Marble 254 by *Rebel Wind-Callowfeenish Dolly*, foaled 1966. breeder Martin Mulkerrins, owner John Brennan

Thunderbolt 178 by *Thunder-Irene Grey*, foaled in 1963, breeder John Brennan

Photo Station House Museum, Clifden

Leam Bobby Finn 297 by *Carna Bobby-Finola* foaled 1967, breeder/owner J.O'Mahoney Meade

Killyreagh Kim 308 by *Carna Bobby-Ballydonagh Kate,* foaled 1967, breeder Col. M. Crichton: with Martin O'Reilly in 1978

Coosheen Finn 381 by *Carna Bobby-Finola* of Leam, foaled 1968, breeder Jack Bolger, owner Lib. Petch

Carrabaun Boy 353 by *MacDuff-Anna Maree*, foaled 1968, breeder M. Daubeny: with John Luskin 1971

Caher Cromlech 433 by *Clonjoy-Sliabh na mBan* 2nd, foaled 1969, breeder Festy Folan: with Willie Murphy in 1971

The Fugitive 368 by *Kimble-Loobeen Lily*, foaled 1968, breeder Patrick Coyne, owner Clair Studdert

Ashfield Bobby Sparrow 444 by *Carna Bobby-Wise Sparrow*, foaled 1970 breeder James Jones, owner Mary McCann

Ballydonagh Casanova 370 by *Checkpoint Charlie-Atlantic Mist*, foaled 1968, breeder T. R.Donnelly, with Lord Killanin and Joe Murphy in 1983

Abbeyleix Owen 496 by *Kimble-Queen of Diamonds*, foaled 1971, breeder Lady de Vesci, with Jimmy Canavan

Loobeen Larry 670 by *Killyreagh Kim-Loobeen Meg*, foaled 1975, breeder R. Tierney: with owner Graham Tulloch

Dale Haze 794 by *Tully Grey-Tulira Bluebird*, foaled 1981, breeder Johnny Lee

Murphy Rebel 696 by *Rebel Wind-Muffy,* foaled 1976, breeder Michael Conneely: with Philip McMahon

Abbeyleix Fionn 810 by *Ashfield Sparrow-Fionnuala*, foaled 1982, breeder Lady de Vesci: with Sean Dunne

Tulira Finn Mac Cool 715 by *Tulira Mairtín-Tulira Heather*, foaled 1977, breeder Lord Hemphill: with Patrick McGrath

Hazy Dawn 849 by *Dale Haze-Castle Park*, foaled 1985, breeder Johnny Lee

Mervyn Kingsmill 762 by *Atlantic Cliff-Mervyn Blue Charm*, foaled 1980, breeder E.B. Berridge: with Ml. King and Donal Kenny

The Kid 877 by *Abbeyleix Fionn-Carabeg Bonnet,* foaled 1986, breeder Michael Walsh

Smokey Duncan 871 by *Westside Frank-Smokey Jane Grey*, foaled 1987: with Josie Conroy

Templebready Fear Bui 880 by *Moyglare Samson-Ballinaboy Jonquil*, foaled 1987, breeder Carol Seigne, owner Dan O'Brien

Moy Hazy Cove 888 by *Hazy Dawn-Windy Cove,* foaled 1988, breeder/owner Johnny Lee

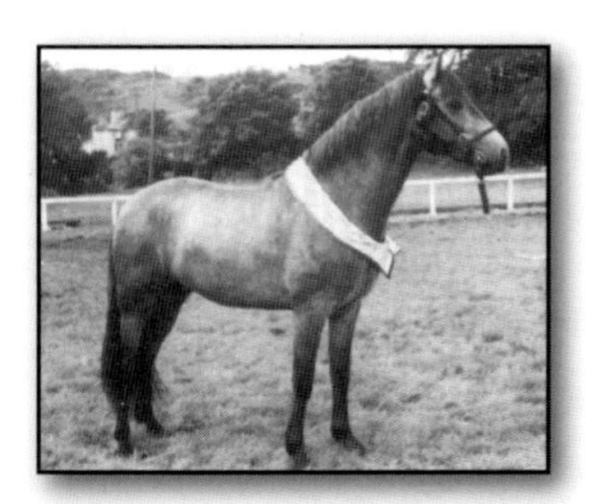

Rocky 914 by *Cuchulainn-Silver Fort*, foaled 1989, breeder Joe Gorham

Village Boy 927 by *Mervyn Kingsmill-Vllage Grey*, foaled 1989, breeder Patrick King: with Tommy O'Brien

Thunderball 948 by *Canal Cormac-Dawn Mist,* foaled 1989, breeder John O'Sullivan: owner Gabriel Murphy

Cloonisle Cashel 980 by *Abbeyleix Owen-Cloonisle Lady*, foaled 1991, breeder Owen Reilly: with owner Eamon Burke

Gleann Rua Maxwell 1030 by *Westside Fred-Moonlight*, foaled 1992, breeder/owner Beatrice Maxwell Murphy: with Lorna Murphy

Garnet Irwin with *Clonkeehan Auratum S 104* by *Naseel-Western Lily, foaled 1963,* breeder M.Lee Norman, with her own mare *Ciro* M 551 by *Silver Pearl Swallow* II, foaled, 1938

Anne 163 by *Rebel*, foaled 1929 owner Tom Folan (John)

Silver Lining 1444 by *Carna Bobby-Speculation*, foaled 1950, breeder Paddy Geoghegan

Golden Gleam 296 by *Adventure*, foaled 1932, owner Dudley McDonagh

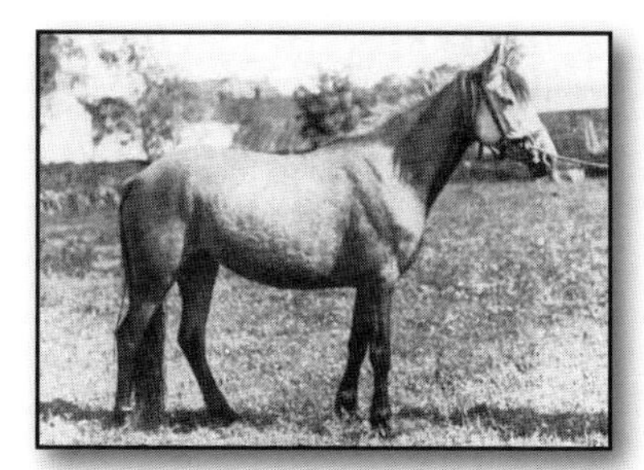

Village Belle 1855 by *Calla Rebel-Village Swallow*, foaled 1956, breeder Patrick King

White Linnet 1060 by *Clough Rebel-White Star* foaled 1944: with owner, Paddy McDonagh, Joe Gorham, Lord Kilannin

Cashel Kate 2030 by *Carna Dun-Rebel Kate*, foaled 1956, breeder John Curran: with Jack Bolger

Flash Judy 2154 by *MacDara-Flash Girl*, foaled 1959, breeder Martin Lee: with Willie Diamond

Belle of the Ball 3122 by *Carna Dun-Glen Belle*, foaled 1965, breeder Christy O'Toole, owner Joe Gorham

Noreen Grey 2287 by *Gael Linn-Rebel Noreen*, foaled 1959, breeder John Joyce, owner Lady Hemphill

Lambay Lassie 3254 by *Clonjoy-Grey Dawn Lassie*, foaled 1966, breeder John Mulkerrins, owner Lord Revelstoke

Heather Mixture of Abbeyleix 2709 by *Clonkehan Auratum-Calla Brown*, foaled 1963, breeder Francis Burke: with Jack Bolger

Abbeyleix Holly 4225 by *Carna Bobby-Abbeyleix Molly*, foaled 1969: with breeder/owner Lady de Vesci

Dun Sparrow 3025 by *Carna Dun-Wise Sparrow*, foaled 1965, breeder John A. Joyce, owner Lady Maria Levinge.

Roundstone River 4746 by *Rebel Wind-Dancing Spanner*, foaled 1970: with breeder/ owner Thomas McDonagh

Village Star 5146 by *Killyreagh Kim-Village Belle*, foaled 1971, breeder Paddy King, owner Henry O'Toole

Sprat Lady 7172 by *Kilgreaney Lad-Kilcloghan Lady*, foaled 1977, breeder Joseph Finn, owner Eamon Hannan

Gloves Misty 6535 by *Carna Bobby-Grey Hop* 2nd, foaled 1974, breeder Thomas Kenny: with owner Eddie Madden

Coosheen Nutmeg 7183 by *Coosheen Finn-Ganty Nutmeg* foaled 1977, breeder Elizabeth Petch

Silver Fort 7281 by *Rory Ruadh-Fort Hazel* and her colt foal *Rocky*, foaled 1975, breeder Dept. of Agriculture, owner Joe Gorham

Kingstown Molly 7604 by *Killyreagh Kim-Park Princess*, foaled 1978, breeder Laurence Maloney, with filly foal *Kingstown Molly* 2nd

Silver Sparrow 6898 by *Abbeyleix Owen-Sparrow Hill*, foaled 1976, breeder Patrick Joyce

Ocean Gypsy 7609 by *Loobeen Lary-Gypsy Moth* foaled 1979, bred by Graham Tulloch: with Joe Gorham junior

Dooneen Star 7871 by *Thunderbolt-Dooneen Grey,* foaled '81 and *Jennifer Rose* 8528 by *Mervyn Kingsmill-Sukie*, foaled '85. breeder/ owner Peter Molloy.

Village Laura 8097 by *Thunderbolt-Village Star*, foaled 1982, breeder Henry O'Toole, owner Padraig Hynes.

Atlantic Peace 7903 by *Tantallon Bobby-Errisbeg Rose*, foaled 1981, breeder/owner Michael Clancy.

Coral Misty 8642 by *Murphy Rebel-Gorteen Misty*, foaled 1986, breeder Pat Mullen: with owner Bobby Bolger.

Owens Lady 8066 by *Abbeyleix Owen Tullabrick Jenny*, foaled 1982, breeder John Joe Toole: with owner Michael Walsh.

Crusheen Connie 9660 by *Corbally Con-Nainsín Bhán* 2nd, foaled 1991, breeder Connie Faherty: with owner Val Noone

Milford Wren 8067 by *Sarsfield-Mervyn Wren*, foaled 1982: with owner John McLoughlin.

Bunowen Beauty 10782 by *Abbeyleix Owen-Irishtown Beauty*, foaled 1995, breeder Noel Sweeney: with owner Padraig Hynes.

Grey Dawn M 1183, foaled 1945, owner R.T. Curley, rider Eamon O'Donohue, Oughterard Show 1949

Patsy Fagan G 58 by *Tooreen Ross-Smokey*, foaled 1960, breeder Murty McGrath, rider Mary Anne Hemphill, owner Lady Hemphill

Oorid Belle M 1394, by *Tiger Gil-June Belle*, foaled 1948, breeder John Walsh: with rider Máirín Cassidy, owner J. Cassidy

Ballydonagh Overdraft S 145 by *Clonkeehan Auratum-Cashel Kate*, foaled in 1962, breeder T.R. Donnelly

Dundrum G (partbred) by *Little Heaven Tb.-Evergood* 1126, rider Tommy Wade in 1962

Waltzing Matilda M 2625 by *Carna Dun-Corrib Lady*, foaled 1962, breeder John Canavan, rider J. Kerins

Photo J. Walshe

Rosmuc Rebel M 1400 by *Lavally Rebel-Rosmuc* in 1957, owner Michael Devane

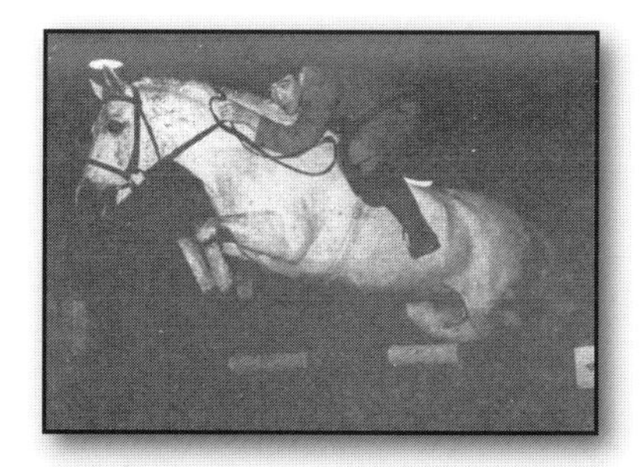

Lough Cutra M 3391 by *Carna Bobby-Tiernee Judy*, foaled in 1966, breeder John Kilroy, rider Noel Healy

Abbeyleix Cypress S 241 by *Doon Paddy-Silver Birch*, foaled in 1966, breeder Viscountess de Vesci, owner Eugenia Murray

Grange Bobbing Sparrow S 623 by *Carna Bobby-Dun Sparrow*, foaled 1973 breeder Lady M. Levinge, rider Caroline Beasley

Tulira Rocket S 343 by Tulira Paddy-Noreen Grey, foaled in 1967 and Patsy Fagan. G 58 by Tooreen Ross-Smokey, foaled 1960, breeder Lord Hemphill

Tantallon Gaye Roberta M 6155 by *Ashfield Bobby Sparrow-Gaye Patra*, foaled 1973, breeder John McCaffrey, owner Juliet Perrin, rider Andrew Perrin

Tulira Rocket S 343 by *Tulira Paddy-Noreen Grey*, foaled 1967, rider Mary Anne Hemphill

Grange Finn Sparrow S 659 foaled 1975, by *Coosheen Finn-Dun Sparrow* breeder Maria Levinge

Ashfield Bobby Sparrow S 444 by *Carna Bobby-Wise Sparrow,* foaled 1970, breeder James Jones: with owner/rider Mary McCann

Pat Aengus G 809 by *Dun Aengus-Village Belle*, foaled 1975, breeder Patrick King, owner Sean Hardiman, rider M. Hardiman

Village Swift G 948 by *Abbeyleix Owen-Village Belle*, foaled 1978, breeder Patrick King, owner Faith Ponsonby

Callowfeenish Mairtín S 846 by *Abbeyleix Owen-Wireless Wave*, foaled 1985, breeder Patrick Walsh, owner Maria Levinge, rider Jenny Essame

Spanish Train G 1044 by *Rory Ruadh-Briarhill Misty*, foaled 1978, breeder Paul Duffy, rider Enda Hannan, owner Eamon Hannan

Garryhack Frederick S 870 by *Lough Dan Easter-Garryhack Pride*, foaled 1986, breeder Joe Day, owner Juliet Perrin, rider Nicola Perrin

Cúchulainn S 789 by *Abbeyleix Owen-Sparrow Hill*, foaled 1979, breeder Peter Joyce, owner James de Courcey, rider, Caroline de Courcey

Robe Island G 1302 by *Island Storm-Robeen Lass*, foaled 1987, breeder Peter McHugh, rider Bijlama Maaike, Sweden

Canal Diane M 8096 by *The Fugitive-Rambling Home*, foaled 1981, breeder Padraig Hynes

Gentle Star M 8815 by *Loobeen Larry-Milford Gazelle*, foaled 1987, bred by John McLoughlin

Canal Lauriston, U.S. stallion by *Callowfeenish Mairtín-Canal Laura*, bred by Padraig Hynes

Rosie Duncan M 10586 by *Smokey Duncan-Slievemore Heather*, foaled 1993, bred by C.Orchard, rider David O'Brien

Doninga Bobby G 1322 by *Ormond Bobby-Tulira Therese*, foaled in 1987, owner Carmel Santry, rider Jean Santry

Castle Comet S 1026 by *Abbeyleix Owen-Castle Dame*, foaled 1994, breeder Henry O'Toole, owner/rider Vanessa Compton

Pangur Pookhaun Rebel G 1520 by Seafield *Pookhaun-Easter Rebel Ruby*, foaled 1990, breeder Eavan O'Dochartaigh, rider William Lalor

Some Man for One Man. G F.810, by *Ashfield Bobby Sparrow-Misty Maiden*, foaled 1994, breeder Peter Meehan, rider Jennifer Lalor

Kilbride Mr. Punch G 1782 by *Abbeyleix Fionn-Joanna*, foaled 1993, breeder Carol Bradbury, rider Jamie Lyttle.

Photo Ruth Rogers

Tulira Roebuck S 1041 by *Earl of Castlefrench-Tulira Heather*, foaled 1995, with breeder/owner Lady Anne Hemphill and Pakie Whelan.

Lishmar Lady Donna M 11600 by *Garryhinch Finn-Lishmar Ginger*, foaled 1996, breeder J.& M. Riordan, rider Thomas Lalor

Western Andy S 1072 G. by *Ardravinna Andy-Western Lady*, foaled 1997, breeder Michael Mitchell, owner Sharon Stockdale, rider Hollie Davis